PEEPING MOT

A MAXWELL

Apogee Press
Berkeley · California
2013

Cover art: *"o" like a bird singing, just for itself* by Erika Lawlor Schmidt, used with artist's permission.

Interior art: detail from *Constantine's Victory over Maxentius* by Piero della Francesca.

Book cover and interior design by Philip Krayna at NKD
www.nkdesigngroup.com

ISBN 978-0-9851007-4-2.
Library of Congress Catalog Card Number 2012956564.

Published by Apogee Press, 2308 Sixth Street, Berkeley CA, 94710.
www.apogeepress.com

1/ Homage to Leo Marks, WWII cryptographer, and author
of the screenplay for Michael Powell's Peeping Tom (1960).

2/ A shorthand for this vertigo of the unfolding epigram:
the experience of an aphorism as it re-engineers the world,
whether cruelly, or paternally, in the model sense of the word,
as a house-husband delighting the orchid in its pram.

1

That poetry is vulnerable to invention.

key: SUSPENDED JUDGMENTS

2

That the derivative work mounts a constitutive defense.

That it will not live as a pejorative.

key: SUSPENDED JUDGMENTS

Of interest in poetry:

- Forensics.
- Unbounded propositions.
- Renovation.
- Priorities.

key: ATTITUDES

What publishing and poetry have in common, fundamentally?

No clue.

It's like a forced marriage of mathematics and cantaloupe.

key: ATTITUDES

No return from the war by doing puzzles. The puzzle is coming home.

I am confident
I am ashamed.

key: PEEPING MOT

Observations in Books

"One sits and is carried into the remote unknown. How well-off I am, really!"

—R Walser, The Little Berliner

key: EXTRACTS

3

That poetry is a commitment to food access.

key: SUSPENDED JUDGMENTS

4

That poetry remains a broad permission.

key: SUSPENDED JUDGMENTS

On Revisionism: 1

Between plagiarism and repetition, there is no substantial relation.

key: EPIGRAMS

On Revisionism: 2

Plagiarism is a moral disinclination. One declines to revert the career.

key: EPIGRAMS

The poem and the publication.

Science and populism.

key: ATTITUDES

Back to the minimum patriarch, a garble among hash marks.

Alive as anything.

key: EPIGRAMS

Manners

What don't I know that I could not say?

What don't I know that I would not say?

key: QUESTIONS

5

That poetry is a controlled vocabulary for what fails to come to
market.

key: SUSPENDED JUDGMENTS

6

That poetry is open to strong propositions.

key: SUSPENDED JUDGMENTS

7.25.10

To small life, the child is ambassadorial, with hiyas to a field mouse,
as though to extend the sure courtesies one cheerfully renews in a
bounded society.

key: LIFE X

On Revisionism: 3

As our case is not new
Let it ring false

To learn, in something like real time,
the exigencies of potential life.

key: EPIGRAMS

"A content affirmation exercise."

Somewhere between irony and forbearance, Steven Farmer turns the perfect phrase to describe the persistent value arbitration within contemporary poetry.

Such valence for this literature that refuses to initialize its variables.

key: EXTRACTS

Limitations

"Bees can remember human faces, but only if they are tricked into thinking that we are strange flowers."

—Harpers Findings, 7.20.10

key: EXTRACTS

7.26.10

Personae are among the lesser gifts to be auditioned in early childhood.

key: LIFE X

What's that?
—*Deeh.*

What's this thing?
—*Deeh.*

In the youngest vocabularies, the sound at the root is a response to the prompt.

Where does this token go when the agreed-upon words crowd it out?

key: LIFE X

Poetry can be made propositional, not to make
a better poetry, and not to marry novelty
to decency or progress, but to argue a life

that remainders nothing short of poetry, an act
of breaking in, and to our own callow house.
To argue a life made not mean by synopsis
but frank and more wild by a typical result.

key: ATTITUDES

- The limitations, or collective punishments, of invention.
- The foundlings of enterprise.
- Henry Vaughan's invocation of a "dirty intelligence."
- The idea of the vernacular; a vernacular of ideas.
- What I will choose to love, and what I will choose to know.

key: ATTITUDES

7

That poetry is open to faithless arguments.

key: SUSPENDED JUDGMENTS

8

That poetry does not care for us in a timely way.

key: SUSPENDED JUDGMENTS

—That poetry is vulnerable to invention
—That invention can proxy for egress
—That poetry can prepare an exception

They think that's what it is:
  the black swan tool.

key: OBJECTIONS

A lie is a virgin pipe to an expensive future.

key: PEEPING MOT

Ashbery's Birthday

Because life is short
We must remember to keep asking it the same question

—"The New Spirit", *Three Poems*

key: EXTRACTS

· · ·

"Momentarily."

That word breaks my heart.

key: EPIGRAMS

In a world of black and white dogs, dirty is indeed the funniest word.

And the kiddos know it!

key: LIFE X

Parenting, not to be confused with curatorship — it teaches asymmetrically.

Like Bell's palsy, the face one places before the child loses its nerve at random, fails to manage, and — self-limiting — reacts to seizure with blind attention.

key: LIFE X

He's delighted, and we want that.

He fails to describe the world in the canonical way, and we want that.

Such even prospects.

key: LIFE X

The terror of an empty box when the adult aspect charms it with an emotion. The comfort of an 'empty' room when its inventories are ready collaborators.

It's animation that's the problem — this space that fills so easily, into which, soft boy, we have brought you so many strangers.

key: LIFE X

- Difficult subjects.
- Plain language.
- Promises.

key: ATTITUDES

Peeping Mot p.3

Bargaining at the counter, the avant-gardist tackles the convoys of scholarship to concoct a personal best — the 'only one of its kind'.

key: PEEPING MOT

The Conceptual Poet and the Hiring Committee

• Invests in genre limits, provided one can violate them.

• Somewhat underdelivers, often dancing around the encounter.

• Tendency to pleonasm, though clearly wants to charm. Hints of personals ad in the LRB.

• Open to traveling for panel appearances.

• Seeks to individuate. Cites collectives as evidence of curatorial abilities.

• Claims not to know who Laurie Anderson is.

• Hyperlinks to allegory (the most repeatable and literary of devices) as evidence of invention.

• Is flexible, underspecifying the 'movement' as necessary, hesitant to commit to self-description should the next conference demand another.

• May read too many back issues of *October* — envious of painting's egress.

• Good at market research, though strangely views literature as emerging market.

- Skeptically references something called "Flarf". *(HC — No one knows what this is.)*

- Provides consistent consumer reporting on previously used theoretical apparatus.

- Definitely willing to travel for panel appearances.

- Possible hire.

key: OBJECTIONS

The Ministry of Information and the "waste product" —
anachronistic, both.

key: PEEPING MOT

8.1.10

Before pitiless animals, it grew larger and larger, the Exhibition on a
string.

Like moralizing to a child, there is no preparation for this — this
dislocation. I'm in the same boat, in the outer ring of the innocent
section.

key: LIFE X

8.2.10

No breeze necessary for the child's mind to lean forward.

key: LIFE X

8.3.10

The happy son throughout the day, in the forecastles of description:
"yellow", "purple", "blue". He pardons me my task-making,
bursting into his tropical outlets, to refresh the elemental world with
the digressions of a visual intelligence.

I don't mind that he comes first. As with Olson: "There is no strict
personal order / for my inheritance."

key: LIFE X

18:24 **Peradventure** there be fifty righteous within the city
18:28 **Peradventure** there shall lack five of the fifty righteous
18:29 and said, **Peradventure** there shall be forty found
18:30 I will speak: **Peradventure** there shall thirty be found
18:31 unto the LORD: **Peradventure** there shall be twenty found
18:32 speak yet but this once: **Peradventure** ten shall be found
24:5 said unto him, **Peradventure** the woman will not be willing
24:39 unto my master, **Peradventure** the woman will not follow
27:12 My father **peradventure** will feel me, and I shall seem
31:31 for I said, **Peradventure** thou wouldest take by force
32:20 will see his face; **peradventure** he will accept of me
38:11 be grown: for he said, Lest **peradventure** he die also
42:4 for he said, Lest **peradventure** mischief befall him
43:12 again in your hand; **peradventure** it was an oversight
44:34 with me? lest **peradventure** I see the evil that shall come
50:15 dead, they said, J— will **peradventure** hate us, and will

key: EXTRACTS

More Manners

"Those who like their discourses what used to be called 'marrowy'
(ie, denunciatory of the opposition) will seek vainly for what they
want in Browne."

. . .

Always the soft boys.
Always the arts.
Always the grapevines.
Always the hirelings.

Publication is not origin.

Where is the entire interview? What is a mistaken belief?

Like at mid-evening, when it's impossible to conceive of a solitary failure, and unmarketability is an accommodating landlord.

"Chain of title." "Talent agreements."

Failure and marketability, interviewed, mistaken for brothers.

key: PEEPING MOT

Any joy is adequate, 'parting hero'.

8.4.10

The father thinks of the son saying to the father:

Any joy is adequate, 'parting hero'.

Momentarily — the future is accommodationist.

We say 'blue sky' as if it were a staple. Not circumambient — an ecstatic fragment.

But a boy in the sleeve of a song points high on cue. Blue, blue, blue! it's a musical accompaniment.

key: LIFE X

"No not now."

A mere alveolar ridge between immanence and withholding.

key: LIFE X

8.7.10

The father is a holdover. Tall, neutral angel, frequently lapsing into
the human.

key: LIFE X

9

That the mien of poetry is eligibility.

key: SUSPENDED JUDGMENTS

10

That poetry stages the struggle to assert an ontology.

key: SUSPENDED JUDGMENTS

What can be told without great impudence?

key: EXTRACTS

• • •

That the "human spirit" is too well-furnished to be crowded into the future.

That the quotation marks are evidence of this.

key: OBJECTIONS

8.8.10

Young thing, I have nothing to remind you of.

key: LIFE X

8.9.10

Save for grammar, young thing, I have nothing of which to remind you.

key: LIFE X

Ætiology of the Snark

Niche is my curse.
Curse is my niche.

key: ATTITUDES

II

That poetry is essentially hostile to invention.

key: SUSPENDED JUDGMENTS

12

That poetry is thankfully mistaken.

key: SUSPENDED JUDGMENTS

Longfellow's Visitors

"A German woman, with a strong accent, called to talk to him about 'The Building of the Ship,' which she was planning to read in public, and which she called 'The Lunch of the Sheep.'"

8.10.10

Reducibly yours.

That the inevitable parental subsidy to the child is chiefly a grammar.

Home is the compose key.

key: LIFE X

To understand Char's sense of *acquiescence*, one must understand what he chose to sentinel: the *sovereignty* of the child.

key: LIFE X

8.13.10

In the background of the visual field, the child is a charged object.
To fix one's attention to him is to fall away from much of the world.

key: LIFE X

8.14.10

At twenty months, the son is the gladdest usher.

key: LIFE X

8.15.10

The father proves nothing by immobility. To join to the occasion, he
must follow, and follow, and follow, and follow.

key: LIFE X

13 Lines on Smallness, from Lucretius

How small can anything be? We know of creatures
So tiny they would seem to disappear
If they were less than half their present size.
How big do you suppose their livers are?
Their hearts? The pupils of their eyes? Their toes?
Pretty minute, you must admit. Well, then,
What about things like those atomic motes
That form the elements of mind and spirit?
Diminutive, to say the least. Nor can we
Find with our finger tips the cause of smell
That clings there from the touch of marigold,
Centaury, heal-all, wormwood, southernwood.
So images move beyond our powers of sight.

key: EXTRACTS

Masanobu Kuno sat down and hand-wrote the lines:

"Do not envy the fathers of others."

"I can't be your horse to ride, but you two be good friends."

"Please be an unbeatable person like your father and avenge my death."

No line from there to here, no line to steer the fingertip across the face, no line to stay the instruction.

key: LIFE X

Behind the "incalculable balances", the cruelty of the parent's corrections. Against the improvisations of the child, he bestows a degenerative gift: personhood.

key: LIFE X

Stevens, the lighthouse.

"We must endure our thoughts all night, until
The bright obvious stands motionless in cold."

key: EXTRACTS

Char, *Leaves of Hypnos:* "Brighten the imagination of those who stammer instead of speaking, who blush the moment they assert something. These are steadfast partisans."

Foundations of Stuttering: [on "utterances having low propositional substance"] Many sources have reported that no stuttering occurs in recitative speaking at various assemblages, such as in certain church rituals. In effect, such performance is choral speaking. Stutter is also said to not be evident in even solo performances of, for instance, the Lord's Prayer, or the Pledge of Allegiance. Regarding this latter group of examples, it should be clear that the propositional value of such expressions is minimal, and that rehearsal and practice must play a crucial role.

* * *

Proposing that the partisan has no need of speech.

key: DEFINITIONS

Domains & Intents: 6

- Propositionality.
- Portability.

key: ATTITUDES

13

That the prototypes of poetry
(the heart, the thing, the idea, spring and / or the rose)
are not evidence of its misapplication.

key: SUSPENDED JUDGMENTS

14

That the poem is the garden of the propositional.

key: SUSPENDED JUDGMENTS

15

That poetry is a wilderness prior to philosophy.

key: SUSPENDED JUDGMENTS

16

That poetry is not here to make these axioms cohere.

key: SUSPENDED JUDGMENTS

U.S. Bonds

In absence of the prerecording, the risk is who might hear.

I want to holler but the town's too small.

key: OBJECTIONS

Anthem

The world is replete, yet there is no end to fiction.

key: OBJECTIONS

Conditions

If one can never concede the defeat of one's own knowledge, one can never be a humorist.

If one can never be a humorist, one can never be perfect.

17

That poetry is forensics, and the field under its scrutiny not Literature, but "the literature".

18

That the literature is inconsistent.

key: SUSPENDED JUDGMENTS

19

That against the literature the poet is an expert witness.

key: SUSPENDED JUDGMENTS

20

That for the poet witness is never incomplete.

key: SUSPENDED JUDGMENTS

The Black Swan Tool

Or, the problem of the **black swan tool**.

Black swan, signifying a statistical exception that falsifies or repudiates a dominant worldview.

Swan tool, used by *recovery servicemen* to 'break into' a vehicle, often to free occupants without agency (eg, a child or a pet) from imprisonment.

The poem as **black swan tool** attempts to engineer an exception, an egress from 'the literature' — from the literary economy or marketplace — yet simultaneously also attempts to break into the vehicle of literary history, or the conceit of a bounded discipline and its progress.

Where aspirant poets desire to invent, but refuse or are impatient with the poem, the tool is the poetic *community*, or the *movement*.

The problem leads frequently to defensive publication — and the vector of poetry is away from publication.

key: DISCOVERY

That poetry is endlessly establishing conditions for fair use.

key: SUSPENDED JUDGMENTS

Value and Disclosure

"The cost of defensive publication can be zero, like a conference paper."

key: OBJECTIONS

Paraphrasing Spicer

That the problem with Red Rock Canyon is that its name is Red Rock Canyon.

What could be meant by 'disputed language'?

What they called for then — when there were names, and not these promiscuous groves.

key: OBJECTIONS

From the inside out, he learns each day that an apple is not a pomegranate.

To bear fruit, he thinks it inside out.

key: LIFE X

All this concern for containment, when the smell of a biscuit lifts every roof.

key: LIFE X

Moment

Late summer, slow chauffeur, bed hovering, night so reluctant to put
me down.

key: AN OPENING

The Defiant Ones

Cara Williams suffers the eternal present:

"All my life I've been waitin' to get away from here. From the mud
gumbo and the loneliness."

Elsewhere, Adorno speaks of a "language without soil."

key: EXTRACTS

10.17.10

"Son" is small, and "small" is a picture of how we care for the small thing.

We all need a massive background.

key: LIFE X

10.21.10

The no-no bird, the turning of the crank. It squeaks, I speak.

And the character of seniority? Described by the ratio of leisure and complaint.

key: LIFE X

Radio Narration on South Africa

"We are giving you this mobile phone so you can be honest about your lives."

Elsewhere, Adorno speaks of a "language without soil."

key: EXTRACTS

10.22.10

Fog delay. It sounds like a weapon, but so does childhood in a certain context.

key: LIFE X

22

That the difference between the poem and the program is the field
of argument.

key: SUSPENDED JUDGMENTS

23

That the difference between the poem and the program is the
expected return.

key: SUSPENDED JUDGMENTS

24

That the world is replete, and repetition merely a spoken word.

key: SUSPENDED JUDGMENTS

10.23.10

A friend's status message always reads: "warm & mandatory."

And I always think, this must be the father's voice.

key: LIFE X

All Good Poems Are in a Suitcase...

...on a baggage rack, on a train, in an anecdote by Hitchcock about the
Scottish Highlands.

Julian Assange listens to the story, but refuses to point to the suitcase.

He's keeping a low cover, twisting his drink tickets between his fingers
as if they were plot coupons in a story vehicle about narrative progress.
He thinks if he can crack the suitcase, he'll have bought himself a new
life.

All good poems are effectively autobiographies of the macguffin.

key: DISCOVERY

Ludwig in the manic phase: "Visual space has essentially no owner."

And that's exactly what I want to know — what *essentially* has an owner.

- This ruthless space without attribution.
- This "disputed language."
- As if one, a prior art.

key: ATTITUDES

10.25.10

You're always young on this cracker earth. Quit angling for the impenetrable precedent. The point is to be thankful for the ducts.

key: LIFE X

The Prior Artist

If I feel *anything*, it's apart from the precedent.

key: AN OPENING

Emerson, on Depletion

Our moods do not believe in each other.

key: EXTRACTS

Toward a Ruderal Sublime

Rooted out — what remains is to our delight.

Three After Racine

Honor, without honey, is a mere malady.

After honey is honor, and then malapropism.

Honor is too fit, yet sweet after the honey of an argument.

key: EPIGRAMS

One After Three After Racine

The fitness of an argument is its grimmer muscle.

One shouldn't come to argue for boundedness, as though for responsibility, unless to come for that laughter at stumbling over its tripwires.

key: EPIGRAMS

25

That at the back of the thought that the poet is defeated by description there is a theory of labor.

key: SUSPENDED JUDGEMENTS

Seven Words into Part One of Thomas Browne's Christian Morals

The word "funambulatory."

Like a silver thread through a laughing key.

key: EXTRACTS

26

That the poem may not observe through decorum.

key: SUSPENDED JUDGMENTS

27

That within the poem a coming to terms may also mean a refusal to
concede.

key: SUSPENDED JUDGMENTS

Gatherings

A thin, crimped stuff — occasional friendship.

key: DEFINITIONS

Mere Words

That minority is the *life* of poetry, and also its cruelty.
We know this, while holding to the curse.

It can't possibly be an epithet — but an essence.

key: ATTITUDES

Conditionals

'Sustainability' suggests permeable defenses, occulted valor and
melancholy.

It's like the final opiate light ebbing in Altman's *McCabe & Mrs Miller*.

key: DEFINITIONS

12.28.10

Dogs are beacons for the fantasist — never reducible to mere appetite and exchange.

A purely transactional relationship with a dog is a draining curse.

key: LIFE X

This Is Our Power

We can scramble the lost.

key: DISCOVERY

Or, as Julia Lupton suggested, negative anthropology could be an account of culture where you subtract human beings. Think of all the artifacts that are not produced by human civilization, like beehives and seashells and things like that. Those could be the objects of a negative anthropology.

—Aaron Kunin, "Banish the World"

★ ★ ★

Regardless of the theoretical subtraction, does this still import a priori a rather optimistic theory of the human?

Where architecture and mechanism retain value as a shadow of some essential human work of event planning — or, say, there is still self-flattery in the plastic spirit and autogenous stones of Kircher and Spinoza.

But more interesting: how the negative anthropologist does taxonomy, which may also be a way of studying religion in this modulo universe. Imagine some clever student beginning to rattle that cage—!

"Which is greater, the umbrella or the face?"

key: QUESTIONS

28

That regardless its antic disclosures, poetry proposes with the velocity of a science.

key: SUSPENDED JUDGMENTS

29

That the poem will not suffer its camouflage.

key: SUSPENDED JUDGMENTS

Two Early Inventions

- Groundlings and mandarins
- Hatchlings from the high blue hat

key: EXTRACTS

That the 'voice' of the poet comes to terms with the principles of
the surface: superposition, original horizontality, lateral continuity.

key: SUSPENDED JUDGMENTS

31

That "the heart of poetry is fatigue" is a model proposition.

That "the heart of poetry is fatigue" must be false for this generation.

key: SUSPENDED JUDGMENTS

32

That the 'voice of the poet' is essentially an argument.

key: SUSPENDED JUDGMENTS

Logistics

That freedom is known as transport while contingency is known as carrying.

I have carried this image to you for so long.

It has transported me to a human element.

key: DEFINITIONS

Propositional Syntax

- I have carried this image to you for so long.
- I have carried this image of you for so long.
- I have carried this image for you for so long.

key: ATTITUDES

33

That the poem is always in its lean-to phase.

key: SUSPENDED JUDGMENTS

34

That the poem is a test against the living.

key: SUSPENDED JUDGMENTS

Rookie Life

Define *answerable*.

key: PROBLEMS

Books thrown to the floor, a test, and protocols scattered. And my 'role' to be corrective, as if the right way lost.

Does forgiveness presume an assignment?

key: LIFE X

Enduring task lists, the 'yous' that accumulate in this spasm of accountability.

You are the low answer. You, this accommodationist.

key: LIFE X

Spinoza Joke

You can't end the sentence with a proposition.

key: PROBLEMS

35

That this poetry must assert its vocabulary *sub specie aeternitatis*.

key: SUSPENDED JUDGMENTS

I'm proposing that thankfulness stands apart from decay. It's not a grooming, or unequal reaction to some splintering oak in the backyard. But it's neither indifferent, this positive, furtive strength.

I'm proposing it, as if it were some eternal notion.

key: LIFE X

Coactivity is the evidence of trust. This son, in his busybody quickening, could hatch societies from all of this sudden planning.

I'm only a bondsman in my heart, and my instruction could never be fair to this exuberance: "first ideas." And not just mine.

key: LIFE X

A motto, out of deep water, and then abandoned to quotation,
as say the 'white creature of chalk pounded', or material sum.
These examples won't explain it, and can't infuse like a drumbeat
these four limbs you're still testing, and testing.

Grow old with me, laboratory.

key: LIFE X

All this language training, and then it's the 'bas-reliefs of earth.'
There's no scale for speaking absent the target. A mass of curls, a
human project, a boy to *speak* to — the mottos exhaust the givens.

And then there's this motto: Candor is the brightest shield.

I want nothing more than direct address, though it delivers nothing
more than a person, and that won't be enough.

key: LIFE X

There is confession and then there is Tripoli.

Which is to say that confession communicates the least.

key: LIFE X

Does humility concede a force, or is it *mere* reluctance?

key: QUESTIONS

This Time It's for Real

Against expression.

Really?

All this endurance of the business and the cruelty to arrive at
reticence— and retention?

A hold-back project, as nostalgic as self-loathing, even where the self
is accidentally yours.

My son is also against expression, mostly anxiously, surprised or
unsure that he is also a container — until periodically he arrives at a
consensus and participates — shitting copiously, and gratefully.

key: PROBLEMS

That despite all this freighted expectancy, it comes wrong in the poem.

key: SUSPENDED JUDGMENTS

Practice

A deep unremitting intelligence, its extensibility, and then the fear of attenuation.

It could be livable.

That despite all this freighted expectancy, it comes wrong.

~~That despited~~

key: PROBLEMS

Actuaries at Peace

Anything is the measure of joy.

The most important thing is not to die.

key: ATTITUDES

Visible Settlements

Hesitation is the actuary of the poem.

All this forsaken urgency, contemplated as risks to a public business,
like nyjer seed scattering across a ledger.

key: PROBLEMS

37

That the poem in its career is primed to the warrant of the
Literature.

key: SUSPENDED JUDGMENTS

38

That poetry is insufficient cover for professional opinions.

key: SUSPENDED JUDGMENTS

—*Peeping mot.*

Looking at you suggests a half-way solution. But then again, you offer me your half-way solution, and there's suggested laughter.

Wry animal face, are you an ethic over there to relieve us from these summing permutations?

key: QUESTIONS

39

That all poems are derivatives.

key: SUSPENDED JUDGMENTS

That every poem is lifeist.

key: SUSPENDED JUDGMENTS

Node Failures

- The transitive relationship between sadness and beauty is refutation.
- *Reachability:* beauty and sadness each fails to disclose it.

key: DEFINITIONS

Further Theories on the Graph

Sadness is wasted on the beautiful. Indifferent to its own capacity, beauty absorbs sadness as if a dispensation.

Beauty is an urelement; it seeks companions, but cannot commit to be compromised.

Sadness is a reduction.

Beauty often volunteers, but rarely communicates.

The moment of the beautiful cannot be depleted, and the career of sadness is toward depletion.

Sadness fails to individuate. Its transitive force exhausts itself in beauty's distended hypothesis, which is unanswerable, save for the wasting challenge of time.

Beauty has too few concerns, whereas sadness is always *evidential*.

The beautiful is wasted on the sad, who seek closure. But beauty, forever eligible, incapable of losing, it has an open face — occupying space without a wasting rhyme.

Where sadness and beauty intersect, all action stops.

key: DEFINITIONS

Share of Voice

The imminent sorrow of the flaccid designator.

key: ATTITUDES

Epigram

We must fight stupidity with color.

. . .

As with the family, or the living, or the poem—

We cannot compare.

Just stop equivocating— you know that

The basic problem is *reachability*.

41

That poetry recapitulates the basic problem of language as forced entry
— or invention.

That the basic problem of language is reachability.

key: SUSPENDED JUDGMENTS

42

That while the language is not transparent, the language may see me
through.

key: SUSPENDED JUDGMENTS

ANDREW MAXWELL is interested in meta-literature and compressed forms. For the last decade, he has worked as a taxonomist and manager of classification and machine learning initiatives at Google in Los Angeles, where he is also a radio DJ and co-directs the Poetic Research Bureau, a valise fiction and reading salon in the arts district of Chinatown. From 1997-2005, he published a journal of poetry and translation, *The Germ*, with Macgregor Card.

Maxwell has released several small collections of poems, lists and epigrammatic writing on the PRB imprint portable, artisanal items meant to pass hand to hand in limited quantity. He typically underwrites his small collections with the simple initial A, as impediment to indexability, and in tribute to other minor/maker poets like David Schubert and Wallace Berman.

OTHER POETRY TITLES
FROM APOGEE PRESS

Maxine Chernoff
Among the Names
The Turning

Valerie Coulton
The Cellar Dreamer
open book
passing world pictures

Tsering Wangmo Dhompa
In the Absent Everyday
My rice tastes like the lake
Rules of the House

Kathleen Fraser
Discrete Categories Forced into Coupling

Paul Hoover
Edge and Fold

Alice Jones
Gorgeous Mourning
Plunge

Stefanie Marlis
cloudlife
fine

Edward Kleinschmidt Mayes
Speed of Life

Pattie McCarthy
bk of (h)rs
marybones
Table Alphabetical of Hard Words
Verso

Denise Newman
Human Forest
Wild Goods

Elizabeth Robinson
Also Known As
Apostrophe
Apprehend

Edward Smallfield
equinox
The Pleasures of C

Cole Swensen
Oh

Truong Tran
dust and conscience
four letter words
placing the accents
within the margin

Laura Walker
Follow-Haswed

**TO ORDER OR FOR MORE
INFORMATION GO TO
WWW.APOGEEPRESS.COM**